D1223135

EXTREME WINTER
SPORTS ZONE

# SNOWMOBILE BEST TRICK

*Jake Carpenter*

Lerner Publications Company • Minneapolis

Copyright © 2014 by Lerner Publishing Group, Inc.

All rights reserved. International copyright secured. No part of this book may be reproduced, stored in a retrieval system, or transmitted in any form or by any means—electronic, mechanical, photocopying, recording, or otherwise—without the prior written permission of Lerner Publishing Group, Inc., except for the inclusion of brief quotations in an acknowledged review.

Lerner Publications Company
A division of Lerner Publishing Group, Inc.
241 First Avenue North
Minneapolis, MN 55401 U.S.A.

Website address: www.lernerbooks.com

Content Consultant: Stephen W. Clark, snowmobile photographer and writer

**NOTE TO READERS: The tricks described in this book are very dangerous. Do not attempt.**

The images in this book are used with the permission of: © Christian Pondella/Getty Images, 5, 7, 13, 28 (top), 28 (bottom); © Jae C. Hong/AP Images, 6; © Chris Council/Aspen Daily News/ AP Images, 8, 18; © Doug Pensinger/Getty Images, 9; © Underwood Photo Archive/SuperStock, 10; © Wayne Davis/Polaris/AP Images, 11; © Andy Cross/Denver Post/AP Images, 12; © Zack Seckler/AP Images, 14; © Gregory Bull/AP Images, 15; © Tony Donaldson/Icon SMI, 16; Stanley Hu/Icon SMI, 17; © Nathan Bilow/AP Images, 19, 29 (bottom); © RJ Sangosti/The Denver Post/ Getty Images, 20–21; © Sbakhadirov/Shutterstock Images, 21 (top); © Nathan Bilow/AP Images, 22; © Aaron Ontiveroz/The Denver Post/Getty Images, 23; © Ryan McVay/Thinkstock, 24; © Steve Mason/Thinkstock, 25; Thinkstock, 26, 27; © David Zalubowski/AP Images, 29 (top).

Front cover: © Doug Pensinger/Getty Images; backgrounds: © kcv/Shutterstock.com.

Main body text set in Folio Std Light 11/17.
Typeface provided by Adobe Systems.

Library of Congress Cataloging-in-Publication Data

Carpenter, Jake.
    Snowmobile best trick / by Jake Carpenter.
        pages    cm. — (Extreme winter sports zone)
    Includes index.
    ISBN 978–1–4677–0759–6 (lib. bdg. : alk. paper)
    ISBN 978–1–4677–1735–9 (eBook)
    1. Snowmobiling—Juvenile literature.  I. Title.
  GV856.5.C37  2014
  796.94—dc23                              2013005252

Manufactured in the United States of America
1 – PP – 7/15/13

# TABLE OF CONTENTS

# CHAPTER ONE

# FRISBY'S FLIP

It was January 29, 2012. Heath Frisby was getting ready to do something that had never been done before. He was going to attempt a front flip at ESPN's 16th annual Winter X Games in Aspen, Colorado. It was the Snowmobile Best Trick competition. Frisby was one of six snowmobilers competing. Snowboarders and skiers often showed off front flips at the Winter X Games. But Frisby hoped to flip while riding a 450-pound (200-kilogram) snowmobile. No one had ever done that in a competition before.

This trick was dangerous. Frisby could break his neck or his back. He could break an arm or a leg. He could even be killed. But Frisby was a skilled rider. He had won the gold medal in Snowmobile Best Trick in 2010. He hoped to win gold again in 2012.

Heath Frisby practices the Indian Air trick that will win him the gold medal at the Best Trick competition at the 2010 Winter X Games.

## HEATH FRISBY: EXTREME SPORTS STAR

Heath Frisby isn't just a star on the snowmobile. He also competes in Moto X Best Trick. This X Games event features riders performing amazing tricks on motorcycles. Many Snowmobile Best Trick stars spend the warmer months riding motorcycles. In fact, Frisby got the idea for the front flip from watching the 2011 X Games. Australian Jackson "Jacko" Strong won the gold medal in Moto X Best Trick when he did the first-ever front flip on a motorcycle at the competition. Frisby thought that if Strong could flip a motorcycle forward, he could do the same with a snowmobile.

The Best Trick competition is a freestyle snowmobile competition. It was only part of the Winter X Games for a few years. ESPN discontinued the event in March 2013. But it was one of the extreme winter sports competition's most popular events. Best Trick usually features eight of the most daring snowmobilers in the world. The athletes take turns racing up a metal ramp. Then they show off their flashiest and most unbelievable tricks to the judges.

Jacko Strong's 2011 front flip in Moto X Best Trick was the first front flip ever landed on a motorcycle in an X Games competition.

Swedish snowmobiler Daniel Bodin's double grab flip won him the gold medal in Best Trick in 2011.

These stunts are wild moves no kid should *ever* try at home. Even Frisby admits to being nervous going into competitions. Injuries are common for Best Trick riders. Daniel Bodin won the Snowmobile Best Trick gold medal in 2011. But he could not compete in 2012. He had broken a bone in his spine while training a few weeks earlier.

At the 2012 Winter X Games, Justin Hoyer crashed while attempting a double backflip. He broke his right arm and left ankle. Hoyer was carried off on a stretcher. Frisby was up next for his first of two runs. He didn't let his nerves get to him. He knew he had to focus. Frisby revved his engine. Then he raced up the 10-foot (3-meter) ramp. Fans held their breath. There was no turning back.

Fans and judges were amazed by Frisby's historic front flip at the 2012 Winter X Games.

Frisby had been practicing this trick for over a month. But he had always landed his snowmobile in a pit filled with soft foam blocks. He had never tried landing a front flip on snow. He didn't want to risk injury before the competition.

Frisby flew up into the air. Then he leaned forward. He tucked his head down as his snowmobile began to flip. Frisby and his sled turned upside down. He was halfway there. But the hardest parts were still to come. He had to hold on to the handlebars and spot a good landing from his upside-down position. Then he needed to spin upright and land his sled in the snow.

The front flip is one of the most dangerous tricks in snowmobiling. The back of the sled whips above the front. The athlete is facing upside down and backward as the sled spins. Then the rider needs to pull the heavy sled all the way around until it's upright again before landing safely on its skis.

The crowd was eerily silent. Frisby hung on. Then, with a hard thump, his snowmobile bounced safely on top of the snow. "Ladies and gentlemen, you just saw history made!" the announcer exclaimed. Frisby raised his fist in triumph. He had won the gold medal. Once again, he was the Snowmobile Best Trick champion!

Frisby receives his second gold medal in Best Trick after his front flip.

# CHAPTER TWO

# HISTORY OF SNOWMOBILE BEST TRICK

Snowmobiles weren't invented for deadly stunts. In fact, some of the first snowmobile riders were doctors. They used snowmobiles to reach patients in snowy areas with unplowed roads.

## The First Sleds

In 1927 a Wisconsin man named Carl J. Eliason gathered a pair of skis, some old bicycle parts, and pieces of a Ford Model T car. Eliason used the parts for an invention he called the snow machine.

Early snowmobiles looked very different from the sleds Best Trick riders use.

In 2000 Edgar Hetteen retraced his 1960 trip across Alaska, using an original Sno-Traveler.

In 1937 a Canadian man named Joseph-Armand Bombardier started a company that still makes motorized sleds. A Minnesota man named Edgar Hetteen later helped found two more snowmobile companies. In 1954 Hetteen, his brother, and his brother-in-law formed a company called Polaris Industries. Hetteen and his partners gathered some spare parts from old farm equipment. They used the parts to create a snow vehicle they called the Sno-Traveler.

Polaris Industries began making Sno-Travelers to sell. But the company got only two orders. Hetteen didn't give up. He wanted to prove how sturdy his machine was. In 1960 he and three others took the Sno-Traveler on a three-week, 1,200-mile (1,900-kilometer) trip across Alaska. The trip showed what Hetteen's machine could do. People started to become interested in using snowmobiles for fun. The United States and Canada were soon covered in trails designed especially for snowmobiling. Hetteen founded another snowmobile company, Arctic Enterprises, in 1963.

Justin Hoyer performs a freestyle snowmobile demonstration at the 2005 Winter Gravity Games in Copper Mountain, Colorado.

## The Next Level

Not all snowmobilers were content with just riding snowmobile trails. By the late 1990s, some people wondered what else they could do on a snowmobile. Motorcycle stunt riders were known for doing amazing tricks in the air. Snowmobilers began to try some of these same moves. It was the beginning of a new sport called freestyle snowmobiling.

In 2000 a new winter sports festival called the Winter Gravity Games began. This was a televised action sports competition for the top skiers and snowboarders in the world. Officials also set up a ramp for snowmobilers. The snowmobilers weren't competing for prizes. But they still wowed the crowd with their amazing tricks. The final Winter Gravity Games took place in 2005.

## TOO DANGEROUS?

Freestyle snowmobilers fly up the ramp at speeds over 65 miles (105 km) per hour. Many snowmobilers are injured attempting freestyle tricks. In 2013 freestyle snowmobiler Caleb Moore was killed when his snowmobile landed on him during a crash at the Winter X Games. It was the first-ever death caused by a crash at the Winter X Games. The tragedy caused many people to rethink freestyle snowmobiling. They wondered if such dangerous tricks were worth the risk. Moore's death influenced ESPN's decision to cancel the Best Trick competition for future Winter X Games.

Levi LaVallee was not seriously injured in this crash during the Snowmobile Freestyle competition at the 2010 Winter X Games.

## Freestyle Takes Off

A professional snowboarder named Jim Rippey decided to try doing a backflip on a snowmobile in 2001. Rippey and some friends built a 25-foot (7.6 m) ramp out in the snowy hills of Utah. Eventually Rippey landed the backflip. A film company called Peak Productions filmed the stunt for a new video series called "Slednecks." The backflip brought worldwide attention to freestyle snowmobiling. Rippey won ESPN's 2001 Action Sports Feat of the Year award for the stunt.

Jay Quinlan rehearses a jump before performing on the Late Show with David Letterman.

Jay Quinlan is comfortable on snowmobiles. His family owned a snowmobile shop on Alaska's Kodiak Island when he was growing up. Quinlan started snocross racing as a teenager. During snocross events, snowmobilers race around a course full of jumps and turns. Quinlan enjoyed the sport. But he wanted to focus on doing tricks off the jumps. In 2003 Quinlan signed up for a new freestyle contest in Jackson Hole, Wyoming. The event was called Red Bull Fuel and Fury. Quinlan completed the first-ever backflip in a competition at the event. The stunt won him a gold medal.

Quinlan agreed to do his backflip on television. He appeared on the *Late Show with David Letterman* in 2005. Quinlan rode his snowmobile out onto a New York City street. Then he did a backflip over two upside-down trash Dumpsters. Millions of viewers saw Quinlan's backflip on television. People became even more excited about snowmobile stunts and tricks.

Early snowmobile daredevils like Quinlan enjoyed flashing their tricks in front of friends and on television. But could their new snowmobile moves turn into a real sport?

### LAUNCHIN' LEVI
On December 31, 2011, pro snowmobiler Levi LaVallee launched himself 412 feet (126 m) over San Diego Harbor. It was the longest snowmobile jump ever recorded. The stunt earned LaVallee a spot in the *Guinness World Records*.

Freestyle snowmobiler Levi LaVallee (left) set a world record when he and motorcyclist Robbie Madison (right) launched themselves over San Diego Harbor in California in 2011.

# CHAPTER THREE

# THE WINTER X GAMES

I n 2007 ESPN added Snowmobile Freestyle to the Winter X Games. In the event, athletes got two runs. Riders had 75 seconds during each run to do as many tricks as they could off a series of jumps. The event was very popular.

Chris Burandt won the gold medal at the first Snowmobile Freestyle competition during the 2007 Winter X Games.

Dane Ferguson does a trick called a twistoff to win gold at the Next Trick competition at the 2009 Winter X Games.

ESPN introduced a new event at the Winter X Games in 2009. It was called Snowmobile Next Trick. In 2010 ESPN changed the name to Snowmobile Best Trick. This competition gives athletes a chance to showcase their most amazing tricks. The competition is limited to eight athletes. But that's enough. Few people in the world have the skills needed to flip a 450-pound (200 kg) snowmobile in the air. Only four athletes signed up for the first competition in 2009. They were Levi LaVallee, Joe Parsons, Jimmy Fejes, and Dane Ferguson. Women have never competed in Best Trick at the Winter X Games.

Best Trick does not require qualifying runs. Athletes are invited to participate in the competition. Because injuries are so common in freestyle snowmobiling, not many athletes are usually healthy enough to compete.

Joe Parsons does a trick called a Gator Wrestler at the Best Trick competition at 2012 Winter X Games, where he won the bronze medal. It takes a lot of practice for Best Trick athletes to master a trick.

## Training

Riders train as hard as they can to get ready for the big show. Because freestyle snowmobile stunts are so dangerous, many pros try tricks on the snow for the first time during competitions. They spend their practice time landing tricks in foam pits.

A foam pit is 10 feet (3 m) deep and sits above the ground. The pit is filled to the brim with soft foam blocks. The riders race up ramps and practice different tricks. Their snowmobiles land in the foam. Then a crane hauls out their sleds. Even trying tricks in the safety of foam can be risky. LaVallee broke a bone in his leg in a foam pit while training for the 2012 Winter X Games.

## *Best Trick Stars*

Best Trick athletes are only in front of the television cameras for a few minutes. But that's all it takes for them to become stars. Athletes use their stardom to help support themselves. Freestyle snowmobiling is an expensive sport. Crashes are common. Pros go through snowmobiles quickly. Companies including Red Bull, Rockstar Energy Drink, and Monster Energy Drink give money to the best-known snowmobile riders. In return, the athletes feature the companies' names on their snowmobiles and gear.

Because freestyle snowmobiling is such a dangerous sport, some riders have trouble finding sponsors. Athletes must sign forms before they compete. The forms state that the athletes understand the risks of the sport and accept the responsibility if they get injured. ESPN required all Best Trick competitors to carry health insurance. But Best Trick athletes also wear special safety gear to help lessen their risk of injury.

Red Bull is one of the companies that sponsors Best Trick athlete Levi LaVallee.

# FREESTYLE SNOWMOBILE SAFETY GEAR

## GLOVES
Riders need gloves with rubber grips. This helps them hold on tight to the handlebars during tricks.

## NECK BRACE
Many freestyle snowmobilers wear neck braces. These help protect riders' necks from serious injuries.

## LEG PROTECTION
Most freestyle snowmobile riders wear knee braces to protect their knees from twisting during landings. Most riders also wear padded shorts and pants.

## BOOTS
Athletes need boots that are flexible enough to move freely but also cushion them during a landing. Freestyle snowmobilers wear sturdy boots with good ankle support.

20

## GOGGLES

Goggles help protect the eyes from flying snow and debris.

## HELMET

Freestyle snowmobile riders always wear helmets. The helmets should cover the whole head and face.

## CHEST PROTECTION

Athletes wear chest protectors with padding from shoulders to waist. The padding cushions a rider's shoulders, stomach, and back.

Justin Hoyer wore the proper safety gear as he practiced for the Best Trick competition in 2011.

LaVallee (above ramp on left) brought his own ramp to use when he nearly landed a double backflip at the 2009 Next Trick competition.

## Inside Best Trick

Best Trick competitions feature up to eight riders. Each rider gets two runs. In some competitions, Best Trick athletes could bring their own ramps to set up for their tricks. In 2013 ESPN changed the rules. The 2013 athletes chose between a 70-foot (20 m) or 100-foot (30 m) ramp. Athletes used whichever ramp they felt would help them get the speed and height they needed for the trick they were attempting.

Cameras follow the riders through their runs. Five judges watch and give athletes a score between 0 and 100. The score is based on the difficulty of the tricks and how well the athletes perform the tricks. The scores from all five judges are averaged. The best score from the two runs counts as the athlete's final score. The athlete with the highest score wins.

The Winter X Games Snowmobile Best Trick competition was the championship for snowmobile stuntmen. It was the biggest event of its kind. But after the 2013 Winter X Games, ESPN made the decision to discontinue the competition in future Winter X Games. The Moto X Best Trick competition was also canceled. ESPN wanted to focus on more established motor sports with a greater number of athletes and more worldwide competitions.

## THE MOORE BROTHERS

Brothers Caleb and Colten Moore stole the show at the 2011 Winter X Games Snowmobile Best Trick competition. Caleb drove during Colten's run. Then Colten hopped on the back of the sled. Colten clung to Caleb's waist as Caleb sped up the ramp. As the sled flipped over, Colten hung on to Caleb. Then Colten kicked his legs down in a move known as an Indian Air. The brothers landed safely, but Caleb had driven on Colten's run, so judges refused to count the trick. Caleb still won the silver medal for his own run.

Brothers Caleb Moore (left) and Colten Moore (right) became known for daring tricks on snowmobiles.

# CHAPTER FOUR

# SAFE RIDES

Freestyle snowmobiling is one of the most dangerous sports around. People should not try the tricks they see pro riders pull off on television. Even snowmobiling on flat ground can be dangerous. Drivers need to be careful. But snowmobiling is a popular family activity. More than 4 million people in the United States and Canada safely enjoy the sport every year. More than 2 million people in the United States and Canada own snowmobiles.

## Learning to Ride

Snowmobile manufacturers make special kid-sized sleds for younger riders. These sleds are lighter and easier for smaller snowmobilers to handle.

Riding a snowmobile is a great way to get outside in the winter.

Kids should take all the necessary safety courses and practice snowmobiling with an adult before riding on their own.

States have their own rules about how old a child must be to drive a snowmobile. Some states allow kids under 12 to ride on public trails as long as they are with their parents or another adult. In other states, kids younger than 12 can ride a snowmobile on their own as long as they stay in their own yards. In most states, kids who are 12 to 16 years old must take a safety class before they can operate a snowmobile on their own. In the class, they learn basic ways to care for their snowmobiles, how to run a snowmobile safely, first aid, and more.

## SNOWMOBILE DOs AND DON'Ts

**Do** wear a helmet, all the time.
**Do** pay attention to signs on and near snowmobile trails.
**Do** ride with a buddy, and make sure an adult knows where you're going.
**Do** slow down to avoid hitting people or animals.
**Don't** drive too fast or over the snowmobile speed limit.
**Do** stick to snowmobile trails.
**Do** stay on the right side of the trail.
**Don't** drive on a frozen lake, river, or pond. The ice can break under the snowmobile's weight.
**Do** carry a first aid kit and food in case of an emergency.

## Snowmobile Safety

The International Snowmobile Manufacturers Association (ISMA) is made up of Polaris, Arctic Cat, Ski-Doo, and Yamaha. These are the four biggest snowmobile manufacturers in North America. The ISMA works hard to promote safe snowmobiling. It has developed a program called Safe Riders! You Make Snowmobiling Safe.

Snowmobilers should always keep an eye out for signs warning about hazards on snowmobile trails.

North America has thousands of miles of trails designated for snowmobiling.

The program has a video, a book, and posters that highlight safety tips. The ISMA even sponsors an International Snowmobile Safety Week to remind snowmobilers to be careful on their sleds.

Some ski resorts have snowmobile programs especially for kids. At Colorado's Vail Mountain, children can ride minisnowmobiles that are designed for kids six to 12 years old. They can hop on and cruise safely around what is called Blizzard Speedway. The course is designed especially for new riders.

There are about 3,000 snowmobile clubs around the world. These clubs are busy grooming trails or organizing family activities. They work hard to keep snowmobiling a safe and fun sport. Freestyle snowmobiling is a fun and exciting sport to watch. But North America has more than 225,000 miles (362,000 km) of snowmobile trails. By following the rules for safe riding, pros and amateurs alike can enjoy wintry fun on a snowmobile.

# SLEDNECK STARS

## HEATH FRISBY

Heath Frisby grew up in Sand Hollow, Idaho. His father liked to compete in snowmobile races. Frisby sometimes tagged along. He also loved watching videos of Jay Quinlan performing snowmobile stunts. Frisby wanted to try some of those tricks himself. When he was 17, he did his first flip on a sled at an indoor snowmobile competition. Frisby won the $25,000 prize. He won the gold medal in Snowmobile Best Trick at the Winter X Games in 2010 and 2012.

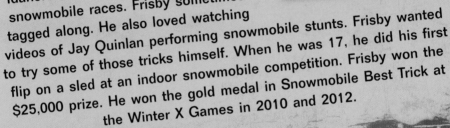

## DANIEL BODIN

Daniel Bodin grew up in a small town in Sweden. Bodin wanted to have fun during the long Swedish winters, so he took up snowmobiling. In 2008 Bodin set a world record. He flew 147 feet (45 m) through the air while doing a backflip. He won the gold medal in Snowmobile Best Trick at the 2011 Winter X Games. In 2012 Bodin broke his neck in a snowmobile crash. He wasn't sure he'd ever be able to ride again. But Bodin recovered from his injury. He came back to win another gold medal at the 2013 Winter X Games.

## LEVI LAVALLEE

Levi LaVallee grew up in Longville, Minnesota. When he was 12 years old, he saved up enough money bagging groceries to buy his own snowmobile. LaVallee started riding it everywhere. He even rode his snowmobile to school. Snowplows cleared the snow off streets and parking lots to form huge snowbanks near LaVallee's home. He used these banks as ramps to do tricks.

LaVallee grew up to become a snowmobile star. In 2009 he nearly landed a double backflip during the Snowmobile Next Trick competition at the Winter X Games. He bounced off the sled during the landing. He won a bronze medal in Snowmobile Best Trick at the 2010 Winter X Games.

## JOE PARSONS

Snowboarder Shaun White may have the most gold medals from the Winter X Games. But Washington State snowmobiler Joe Parsons is next in line. Parsons has won 12 medals in snowmobile events at the Winter X Games. He won the bronze medal in Snowmobile Best Trick in 2012. At the 2013 Winter X Games, Parsons spun his body around while flying upside down. Then he landed backward on his sled. Parsons called his trick the Gator Hater. It won him the silver medal. Parsons also holds two world records for snowmobile freestyle tricks.

# GLOSSARY

**AMATEUR**

someone who participates in an activity for fun without expectation of payment

**DAREDEVIL**

someone who participates in risky activities

**FREESTYLE**

a style of snowmobiling where athletes do tricks instead of race

**PROFESSIONAL**

someone who participates in an activity as a job for payment

**RUN**

a trick or series of tricks done at one time

**SPONSOR**

a company that helps support an athlete with money or parts

# FOR MORE INFORMATION

## Further Reading

Bailer, Darice. *Snowmobile Snocross*. Minneapolis: Lerner Publications Company, 2014.

Older, Jules. *Snowmobile: Bombardier's Dream Machine*. Watertown, MA: Charlesbridge, 2012.

Sommers, Michael A. *Snowmobiling: Have Fun, Be Smart*. New York: Rosen, 2003.

## Websites

**ESPN X Games**
http://espn.go.com/action/xgames
The official website of the X Games. The site has pictures of the stars and videos of their medal runs.

**International Snowmobile Manufacturers Association**
http://www.gosnowmobiling.org
This website has loads of information about snowmobile trails, clubs, safety classes, and clothing.

**Snowmobile Hall of Fame and Museum**
http://www.snowmobilehalloffame.com/index.html
This website tells the history of snowmobiling, including pictures and stories about legendary stars.

# INDEX